RECOVERY

Life After the Loss of Angela

GUGLIELMO

RECOVERY

Life After the Loss of Angela

979-8-88945-162-4 paperback
979-8-88945-163-1 ebook
979-8-88945-164-8 hardback

Printed in the United States of America.

Brilliant Books Literary
137 Forest Park Lane Thomasville
North Carolina 27360 USA

Contents

Chapter 1
HOSPICE

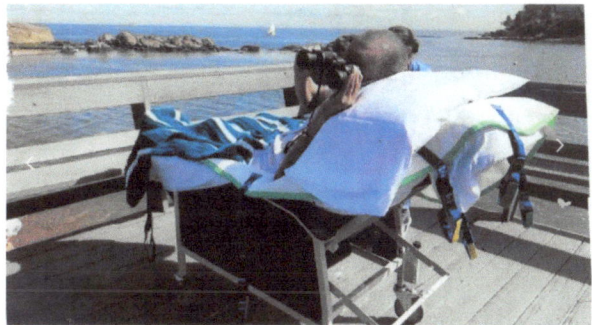

Angela was at home with me, hospice was coming to care for her there. One night she was not feeling very well, so I decided to take her to the emergency room.

The doctor who examined her, informed me that in his opinion, she had just three hours, perhaps, three days at the most to live, and he was admitting her to hospice care.

The thought of losing her was now bearing heavily on my mind.

Once she was settled in hospice, I couldn't bear the thought of being separated from her.

I asked for permission to stay with Angela. Gratefully they allowed me to stay and provided me with a mattress next to her bed. For this accommodation, just to be with her made me very happy.

We were still together, for whatever time God would allow.

Two months passed and one night I heard her stirring. She was sitting up in bed with her arms reaching upward as if she saw something or someone.

I called for the nurse, she came and gave Angela some medication to calm her, but in a few seconds she passed in my arms.

I was dazed. Reality set in like a ton of bricks. For the first time in my life, I knew what it felt like to be in shock.

I called my children, and then proceeded to empty her locker and head home.

Chapter 2

HOME TO AN EMPTY HOUSE

When I reached our home, reality came crashing down on me. I was ALONE. Angela and I had never spent more than two weeks apart in fifty six years of our marriage.

Completely heartbroken, sobbing until there were no more tears. What happens now? What do I do without her?

Funeral arrangements have to be made, keep yourself together. Think about the kids. Don't let them see you like this, I said to myself. Angela wouldn't want you to be so distraught. All these thoughts were spinning in my head. My heart was broken, beyond repair.

I had to keep it together, so much to do and nothing but time to do it in.

The thought of the home we had together in Florida, how happy we were, all gone now just a memory. Nine years of total happiness and bliss, never to return.

The funeral came and I found out just how many people loved Angela. Friends from her childhood came to pay their respects, telling me how much they loved my wife.

At the church I tried to give the eulogy, my throat just closed and I could not continue. Donald, my grandson continued on from my notes. I just couldn't.

Reality had set in, Angela was gone. But so deep in my heart not ever forgotten.

Chapter 3

REALLY ALONE

Couldn't get much sleep. Memories were spinning in my head every minute of the living day.

Depression, which was foreign to me, became my constant companion. Why am I here? Why did Angela have to suffer so much? I should have been the one to go first. These questions ran through my mind repeatedly.

My children took this loss extremely hard. They needed me now more than ever, to be there for them was a struggle, but I had to be the rock. This was also a drain on me keeping my mourning on the back burner.

Time went on and they all fell back into their routines, working, and making a living. The loneliness closed in on me with such heaviness, coping was almost impossible.

A grown man losing self control, not able to accept the fact that Angela was gone and not coming back ever was hard to comprehend.

My daughters were concerned and were making all kinds of suggestions, trying to cheer me up. Believe me I tried until finally I learned about a study being conducted regarding depression.

I called and was blessed with the fact that this study offered counseling, and medication for depression.

It was the beginning of a road to recovery.

Chapter 4

BEREAVEMENT

One of my friends suggested that I join a group of other people trying to cope with their loss.

A church in a nearby town had such a group and I reluctantly joined.

My first impression was one of amazement at the length of time that had passed in some cases, many years had gone by since their loss.

The feeling of not being alone and maybe being foolish, overcame me and as each meeting progressed, I could feel a sense of comfort knowing that I was not alone in my grief, losing some of my feelings of shame, at not being able to cope.

All these folks had loved and lost their partners, or their sons or daughters, mothers or Fathers. The pain was universal.

At the end of these sessions, my outlook seemed to improve. The guilt of being still alive, and alone seemed a little less of a factor.

I also learned that keeping busy was most important, for my well being, and recovery.

The thought of taking my own life had been very much on my mind, but being a Catholic kept that thought at bay.

To lose any chance to join Angela would not happen, since if I took my life there would be no place for me to be with Angela in paradise.

Being a part of this group helped me a great deal on the road to recovery.

I will always be grateful for that experience.

Chapter 5
WHAT TO DO NOW

When Angela and I lived in Florida, I always thought I would pass first.

I suggested that Angela should have a pet, preferably a dog, for company. Angela did not want to hear of it, "bring a dog home, and out you both go".

One day at breakfast she was reading the paper. She proclaimed "Oh look Hon, there's a Boston Terrier puppy for $400.00, isn't that good?" "Back home they want $1200.00". "Let's go check it out".

Off we went. I couldn't believe this was happening. Angela had been so adamant about ever getting a pet.

The puppies were in a private home. When she saw them, her heart melted.

And guess what? She picked one out, a little female and named her Bella Mia.

Bella soon had Angela wrapped around her little paw. This whole scene blew me away. Before I knew it, Angela was playing with Bella in our pool, and knitting sweaters for her. She was a happy addition to our family.

After Angela passed, Bella was my greatest comfort, I adored her.

The thought of losing Angela was bearing down on me. (Pancreatic Cancer is a death sentence), I was beside myself with worry. I tried to find something to keep me occupied, and from losing my mind.

From somewhere the hobby of making costume jewelry came to mind.

Chapter 6
KEEPING BUSY

Keeping busy I think was the key to coping with my loss. I could never feel good the way I did with Angela by my side, but what can I do?

Somehow, some way, from deep within my heart and soul, came forth the creation of "I Take Thee Angela". Never thought of poetry as part of my life but it just came pouring out and was my gift to Angela, her legacy.

In 2012 "I Take Thee Angela", was published, five years after her passing.

The message I hope, is for others to see how rewarding, love and sharing love can be.

It was such a blessing to hear the comments that those who read my book made, and how it was a positive influence on their lives.

The jewelry that I created was a daily chore, and that kept me occupied.

Bracelets, necklaces, earrings. Gave me such a sense of satisfaction when each piece was finished.

I had a website created hoping to deplete the supply I had created, not wanting to leave a room full of jewelry for my kids to deal with after I go to be with Angela. It hasn't been what I had hoped for, people didn't look up the website at all.

Along with "Keeping Busy". I heard of fairs where Vendors display their merchandise for sale. Long hours, not very profitable, but offered the opportunity to meet some great people and to socialize It has been a great experience.

Chapter 7
DAY BY DAY

Angie and Bellamia

Bella Mia was such a love and as my companion, brought me so much joy everyday.

One day I was on the internet and there was a tiny Boston Terrier named "Angie" up for adoption. Was this somehow a message for me? Did I really need another friend?

Drove to Long Island, and met "Angie", it was love at first sight. All the way home, hoping that Bella would like her too. They became the very best buddies.

Little Angie became my shadow and was such a loveable little girl. After a while Angie began to have seizures.

Bella Mia was aging right before my eyes. Never entered my mind that she too would get sick, and leave me.

At twelve years of age, Bella refused to eat, did not want to go for our walks, became very lethargic. At the vet they advised euthanasia.

"Oh, it's just a dog". You have little Angie, that's life. This is what I heard over, and over again.

She was not just a dog, she was part of my family. It was another blow. Was this Karma, I had little Angie to be with, and a joy she was. Wanting to be with me every minute. My protector.

Then, Angie began to have seizures, she would faint and her body would shake all over. I rushed her to the vet, and devastation followed me again.

Angie had a brain tumor and there was no choice but to euthanize her. It broke my heart, she was so young. Bella Mia grew older and with me for twelve years. The day came for me to say goodbye and let her go, felt alone again and I drowned in grief again.

Another devastating loss. These beautiful little girls were such a saving factor for me in my grief.

I have always been a caretaker and they needed me but I needed them more. Another of my angels was not with me anymore

Chapter 8

LIFE GOES ON

These little beings filled a void that had been so hard to endure. Without them, my life would have been just an empty shell.

Fate had chosen to take them from me, Bella was gone, little Angie no longer a part of my life.

Not all people appreciate the joy that a pet can bring. They seem to always understand the time when you need them most.

Always there for you, no matter what your mood, they know just how to act or what to do at just the right time.

I have found that I was hooked on this particular breed, maybe because my wife Angela had first brought Bella into our lives.

Boston Terriers in my case have always displayed a tenderness that immediately wins over your heart and created a feeling of love and warmth that cannot be ignored.

My love's are gone now, but what they gave me during a time when we needed each other will always be in my heart and mind.

What do I do now? Older and without their companionship? Life must go on.

Chapter 9
ANOTHER MOVE

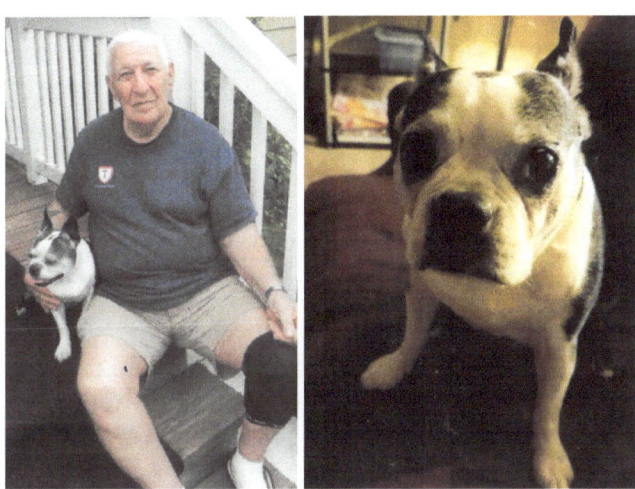

My home was becoming too much to care for. Getting on in years, made cutting the grass too much and painting harder and harder to perform. I didn't need six rooms for just me. Decided to look for a condominium.

Without my little friends as company, depression loomed over me daily.

Mill Pond Village had a condo for sale a small kitchen, living room dining room combination and two bedrooms and bath.

Perfect for me, but again it was just me. Being alone again was very hard to adjust to. I had been blessed with the loving companionship, of Bella Mia, and Angie wonderful company and they had needed me, but I needed them more than I realized.

I contacted the North Eastern Boston Terrier Association. My heart was open to rescue another sweet girl. I was getting on in years so a puppy was out. I wanted an older friend who needed a home.

After the death of my girls, I was getting older but being alone again was hard to take, so I rescued "Ada", another Boston Terrier.

These beings filled my life with love and joy.

Unless you are a canine lover you cannot imagine how much they grow on you and fill your life with such joy. I think that was the reason I was hooked on this breed, so full of love and caring

Asking little in return for your attention.

For four years we shared love and companionship until one day Ada began spitting up non stop. Took her to the emergency vet.

They would not let me see her the first day, but I could not go another day without seeing her. When they brought her to me. She could not even stand, drugged, and definitely not the girl I brought to them for help.

Whatever they did she was in a terrible state. I couldn't see her like that and I held her in my arms as they administered their needles.

To this day I believe they brought about her demise.

Chapter 10
THE PROMISE

Shortly before her passing, Angela, in a very serious mode, approached me with a request, a request that was a challenge that I would not have ever expected.

Angela said, " Promise me you will keep this family together".

At the time, my children were in marriages, or relationships, that were not in the best circumstances.

Reluctantly I agreed, there was nothing in this world that I would have denied her.

I would do my very best to keep my promise, it was all she asked of me.

The emotions and aftermath clearly showed just how much their mother meant to them.

I was surrounded by broken hearts. We all would be in need of mending.

As time went on, and their daily life seemed to get back to normal, contact with me became less, and less.

Angela's request lay heavily on my mind, it was my challenge, for me, and me alone.

Each day I made it my business to call each of my children, spending as much time as possible on each call.

My children are gems and they come with different stories as well.

Angelo, seemed to be my greatest challenge. We had never been as close as I would have wanted to be.

Chapter 11

ANGELO

One of the hardest working men I have ever known.

The problem we had here was not with my son,but for some reason, the chemistry with his wife, left something to be desired.

No matter how hard I tried, warmth never happened.

Without getting into personal details, after sixteen years of marriage, it was over.

The house, all assets, Angelo surrendered to his spouse, so much so , that he was living in his truck.

After a while he was able to live with his sister, Geri, for a while. That worked out for a while, but then he was given a room in his brother Philip's home.

(Since I am discussing their very private lives and reasons for decisions, I cannot bring myself to reveal factors that are really private and not relevant to this story)

Angelo was devastated by his circumstances and was again living in his truck. I was not aware of his dire situation.

When I did learn about it, I asked him to please come live with me. At first he was reluctant to move in but then relented.

Being Angelo, he insisted on helping pay for his keep, and he did just that.

As time went on, I was very happy to see him get on his feet, but most of all our relationship grew beyond my expectations.

A mutual respect and my admiration for my son continued to grow day to day. We eventually moved to the condo on Mill Pond Road.

Angelo was a blessing, age was creeping up on me and he did so much for me. I am truly grateful.

Seeing him on his feet and thriving, I very carefully suggested that he might want to be more independent.

We researched a place for him to live, just ten minutes from me.

One day, he said to me "Dad, you are my best friend". My heart was filled with such pride and happiness.

Now living on his own we are in constant contact.

Chapter 12
GERI

My daughter Geri was our second born. I can remember Angela saying "This time I am waiting before you take me to the hospital, I am not going through a long labor like when Angelo was born".

True to form, we just made it in time, Geri, was not going to be denied. She came so quickly that I was in the right place at the right time, able to see her right after the birth. There was my beautiful daughter.

(At the time no one from the family was allowed in the birthing room, not even the father.)

As she grew, she proved to be a very precocious child, independent, very independent and smart as a whip.

All her life as she grew up she always took care of herself. She excelled in school and was always financially stable.

We were in awe as we observed the wonderful way she raised her children. A son Donald was born first, followed by a sister Mia.

Angela was thrilled and became a doting grandmother. Angela often watched the grandchildren while Geri worked.

Mia has now made me a great grandfather twice over the birth of a son Roman, now two years old and the recent birth of Matteo made it a double.

Each day Geri calls me with a cheery, "Checking in Dad "These calls mean so much to me, I am there for her and she is there for me.

How many fathers are as lucky as I am?

Chapter 13
PHYILLIS ANN

Phyllis was our middle child. A very sweet loving girl. Very shy and totally void of self esteem.

You would never notice her inner feelings since her way was to hide her unhappiness.

Phyllis was very much like her mother, Angela in so many ways, even in her looks, she was the picture of her mother.

When she was eighteen years of age she met the man who would later become her husband. When Angela and I met him we were not very impressed, there was something about him that raised a red flag.

Phyllis on the other hand seemed to be happy to be in a relationship.

John (not his real name) convinced my daughter to move to New Jersey since his commute to be with her was too much of a burden to him.

I begged her not to go, telling her that if he really loved her he would go to the moon and back. Phyllis did not listen and entered a life with someone who was a control freak. He did all he could to keep her from her family and friends.

This worked for a while, but her love of family and friends would not be denied.

Her privacy, as that of all my family, is of the most importance to me so I will not venture too deeply into the events of her personal life except to say that for many years she and our family endured much heartache and problems.

What I can say is that Angela and I were always there for her with support and whatever help she might have needed.

The important thing that I can say is that after years of heartache and worry Phyllis turned her life around and we were most grateful to have our daughter back and happy.

Our kind, sweet, caring loving daughter had never changed, she was still the sweet, loving caring person she had always been.

Chapter 14
PHILIP

Our son Philip was our last to be born. Now our family is complete. The birth went well, but little did we know what lay ahead. Something was not right with this baby boy. All we thought was that he was such a good baby. All he wanted to do was sleep.

At two months old, our doctor, at his usual visit, informed us that Philip was born with a hole in his heart.

In those days open heart surgery had not been perfected. Our doctors told us he had been monitoring Philip's condition, and had made an appointment at New York Hospital Pediatric Cardiac Clinic.

For four years we watched and waited, taking such care for Philip as we were directed. One day a letter came from the New York Hospital that they had perfected an open heart procedure for Philips' condition and scheduled a date for surgery, on April 4,1966.

All we could do was pray that all would go well, and thank God it did.

There were mixed emotions to see this little boy after surgery so pale he blended into the pillow where he lay.

Recuperation was long and tedious especially for Philip, but he did amazingly well.

The surgery saved him and he could now live a normal life.

To see him today one would not believe he had undergone life saving heart surgery. A strapping young man he grew up to be.

Part of our happy loving family.

Chapter 15

A PROMISE KEPT

Angela as I mentioned previously, as her last wish " Please keep this family together.

On Christmas Eve, my whole family was there together for only the second time since Angela's passing. That was too long a time.

The first time was when my children surprised me with a 90th birthday party, then on Christmas eve.

I know Angela was there in spirit, seeing us all together, happy and enjoying the moment must have made her smile. Christmas Eve all together.

I cannot take all the credit for this momentous occasion, since my daughter Phyllis was the one who with lots of hard work made this gathering possible.

Phyllis, the most thoughtful, kind, loving daughter, created an evening that made me very proud.

My whole family was there. I met my second born, great grandson, Matteo for the first time, it was the highlight of the evening.

Both my daughters, Geri and Phyllis, followed in their mother's footsteps and are both fantastic cooks.

Everyone brought something in the way of their favorite dishes, and it was a feast to remember.

Living to be 90,. Is almost unbelievable, and also surviving the loss of my wife for so many years, is hard for me to fathom.

As lucky as I am, the most beautiful blessing is to have this family, born from the love of my life, Angela.

This Christmas was one filled with love and joy. My life has been a good one. Not only was I blessed with a love that has sustained me for years, but I have been privileged with the ability of seeing my children all grown and living their lives as they choose.

Thank you Phyllis for being you, and for helping to make a promise come true. You are truly loved.

A promise kept, is like a diamond found.